BARKER CREEK®

"WOW"ers

Text and Illustration
Copyright © 2016
by Barker Creek Publishing, Inc.

Graphic Designer:
Vickie Spurgin

Printed in the USA

ISBN: 978-1-928961-43-7
Item Number: LL303

BARKER CREEK

P.O. Box 2610
Poulsbo, WA 98370
www.barkercreek.com
800.692.5833

92 Reproducible Awards & Templates

See Barker Creek's full line of Award-Winning Titles including:

Reading FUNdamentals™ Series

Very, Very Vocabulary

Picture This! Graphic Organizers

Sticker USA Activity Book

Glad to be Me

"Zoo"bilee

Giddee Up! Round Up!

Tails of the Sea

Falling Into Colors

The following E-Books are available at
www.barkercreek.com

Homonyms, Synonyms & Antonyms

Bunches of Bugs

ABC, 123 and the Coconut Tree

Under the Bigtop

… and many more!

Welcome to "WOW"ers!

Kids Love to be Rewarded

You'll find many fun ways to praise your students or your own children with these reproducible awards and certificates.

About This Book

"WOW"ers includes a wide variety of reproducible awards and certificates to recognize and celebrate special achievements and a job well done. Refer to the Table of Contents for a complete list of the awards included in this book. The awards listed on pages 36 to 40 celebrate special days including several popular holidays, birthdays and 100th Day. Use the templates on pages 41 to 47 to create your own awards.

How to Use This Book

The awards and certificates in this book are designed to be photocopied on white or colored paper. For added durability, copy them on cardstock. Each certificate includes room for the recipient's name, date awarded, presenter's signature, and, when appropriate, a brief explanation of the job well done.

2

TABLE OF CONTENTS

TABLE OF CONTENTS
(continued)

Reading Award

Name_____

Date_____

Award Given For _____

Signed _____

Keep your imagination
blooming...READ!

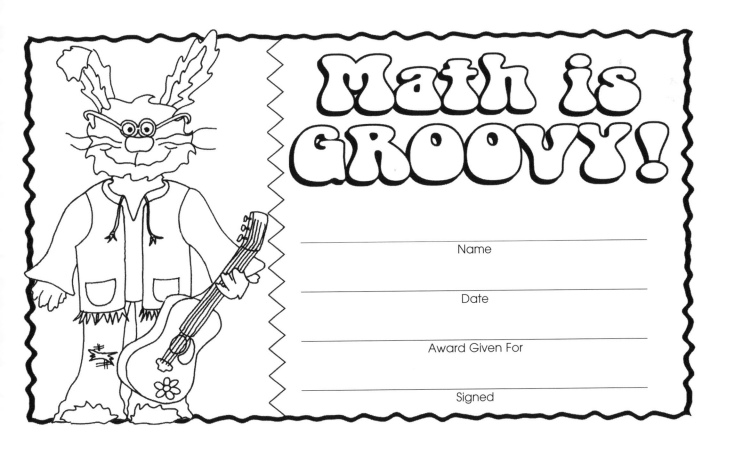

Math is GROOVY!

_____
Name

_____
Date

_____
Award Given For

_____
Signed

BRAVO!
My hat's off to you!

_____
Name

_____
Date

_____
Signed

YOU'RE A CLASS ACT!

_____
Name

_____
Date

_____
Signed

WOW!
You lost a Tooth.

Name _____

Date _____

Signed _____

Thanks for Your Helping Hands Today!

Name _____

Date _____

Award Given For _____

Signed _____

Name _____

did a really "COOL THING" today!

Date _____

Award Given For _____

Signed _____

You pulled through in a CRUNCH... Thank you!

Name _____

Date _____

Award Given For _____

Signed _____

PLACE MINIATURE
NESTLE'S® CRUNCH
BAR HERE

A job well done. You finished!

Name _____

Date _____

Signed _____

Note: For an extra treat, attach Nestle's® Signature Treasure Candy to the treasure chest award.

8

"WOW"ers™ ©2016 www.barkercreek.com

_____
Name

was "ALL EARS" today.

Thanks for being such a good listener.

_____
Name

_____
Date

_____
Award Given For

_____
Signed

I'm really proud of you,

_____
Name

"You stuck your neck out" today when you

_____
Award Given For

Thanks!

_____
Date

_____
Signed

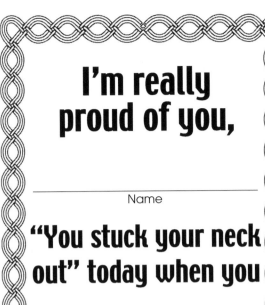

Name_____

shoots for the stars during
_____ time.

Date_____

Signed_____

_____ was caught today
"BEE"ing a good friend.

Date_____

Signed_____

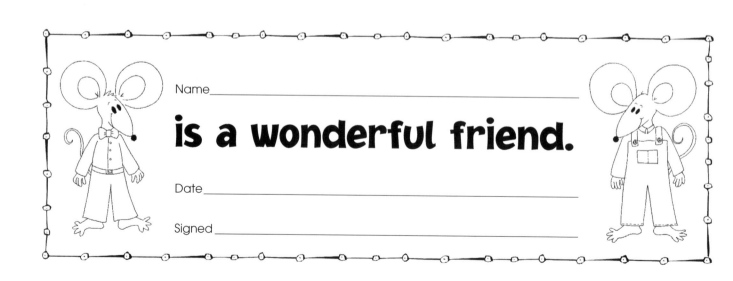

Name_____

is a wonderful friend.

Date_____

Signed_____

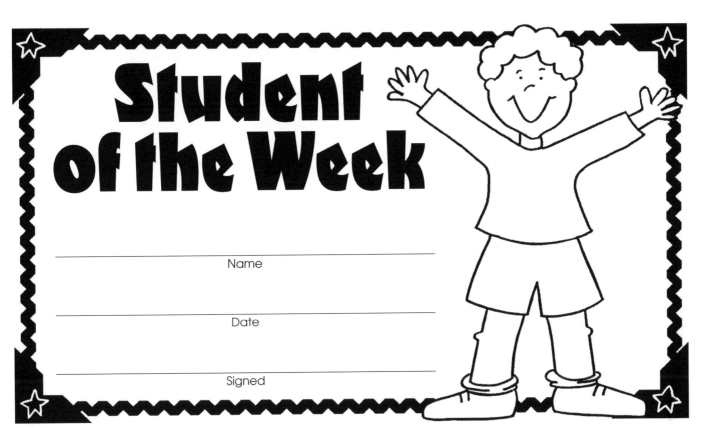

Student of the Week

_____
Name

_____
Date

_____
Signed

Student of the Week

_____
Name

_____
Date

_____
Signed

★ You're Bright!

Great thinking in class today!

Name_____

Date_____

Signed_____

Self Manager Award

Name_____

Date_____

Award Given For _____

Signed _____

Leadership

On Time   On Task

Responsible   Caring   Helpful

I learned something new today!

Name _____

Date _____

Award Given For _____

Signed _____

Zooming Through School!

Great Progress Award!

Name _____

Date _____

Award Given For _____

Signed _____

Good Attitude Award!

Name_____

Date_____

Signed _____

You Did It! Great Accomplishment

Name_____

Date_____

Award Given For _____

Signed _____

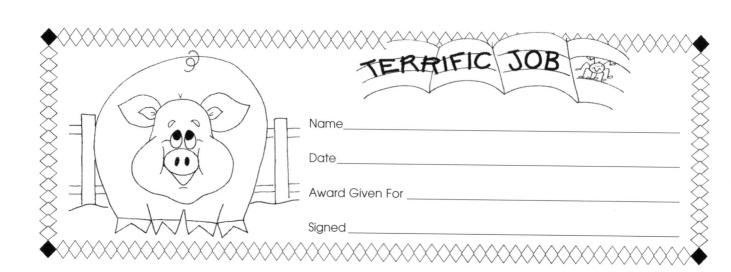

TERRIFIC JOB

Name_____

Date_____

Award Given For _____

Signed _____

You are a ☆ STAR ☆ !

Name_____

Date_____

Signed_____

Wow!
You Can Tell Time.

_____
Name

_____
Date

_____
Signed

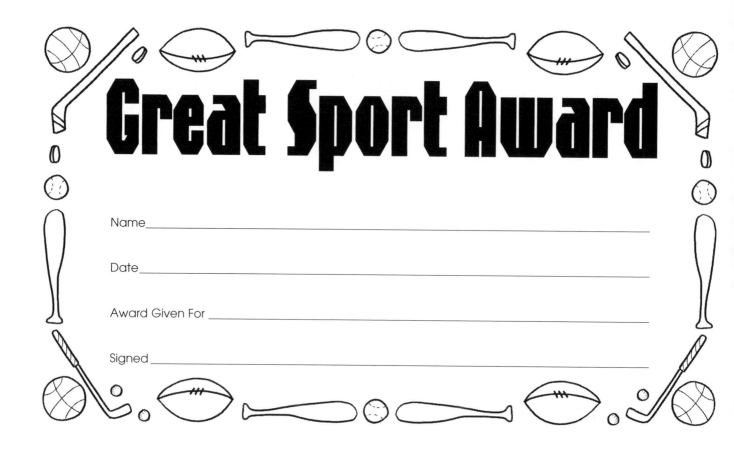

Great Sport Award

Name_____

Date_____

Award Given For _____

Signed_____

Here's the BUZZ!

_____
Name

was a good listener today.

_____
Date

_____
Signed

Sharp Writer AWARD

_____
Name

_____
Date

_____
Signed

_____ **was the**
Name   **Cat's Meow**
                         today

_____
Date

_____
Award Given For

_____
Signed

WELCOME TO OUR CLASS!

Name _____

Date _____

Signed _____

A "Dog-Gone" Good Job!

Name_____

Date_____

Award Given For _____

Signed _____

Here's something to bark about!

Name_____

Date_____

Award Given For _____

Signed _____

Your handwriting is so "PURR"-fect!

Name_____

Date_____

Signed _____

18

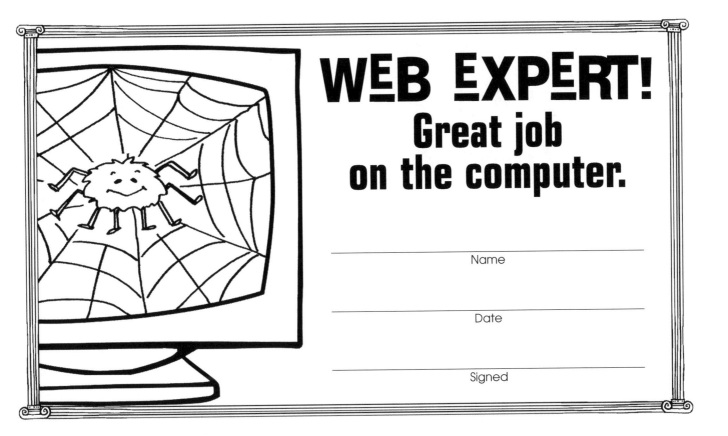

WEB EXPERT!
Great job on the computer.

_____
Name

_____
Date

_____
Signed

Welcome to _____ grade.

We're WILD about you!

Name_____

Date_____

Signed_____

You were an ANGEL today!

Name_____

Date_____

Signed_____

A+
Field Trip Behavior!

_____
Name

_____
Date

_____
Signed

SUPER EFFORT!

_____
Name

_____
Date

_____
Award Given For

_____
Signed

Your Performance Was Outstanding!

_____
Name

_____
Date

_____
Signed

GREAT GROUP WORK!

You worked together. Thank you!

_____
Date

_____
Signed

Congratulations!
You did your best.

_____
Name

_____
Date

_____
Award Given For

_____
Signed

Bueno!

_____
Name

_____
Date

_____
Award Given For

_____
Signed

★ PERFECT ATTENDANCE!

Name_____

Date_____

Signed_____

You are a LIFE SAVER!

Name_____

Date_____

Signed_____

Note: Attach Lifesavers® to the corners of the life saver award.

"WOW"ers℠ ©2016 www.barkercreek.com

23

SUPER JOB!

You know your ABC's!

_____
Name

_____
Date

_____
Signed

WOW!
A perfect paper!

Name_____

Date_____

Signed_____

A+

LADIES AND GENTLEMEN: ANNOUNCING A GREAT JOB TODAY!

By _____

For _____

Date _____

Signed _____

Nothing "Fishy" about it...
you deserve the
READING AWARD!

CURIOUS CLOWNFISH

Name_____

Date_____

Signed_____

You made me SMILE today!

Name_____

Date_____

Signed_____

SCIENCE PROJECT AWARD

Thanks for participating!

_____
Name

_____
Date

_____
Signed

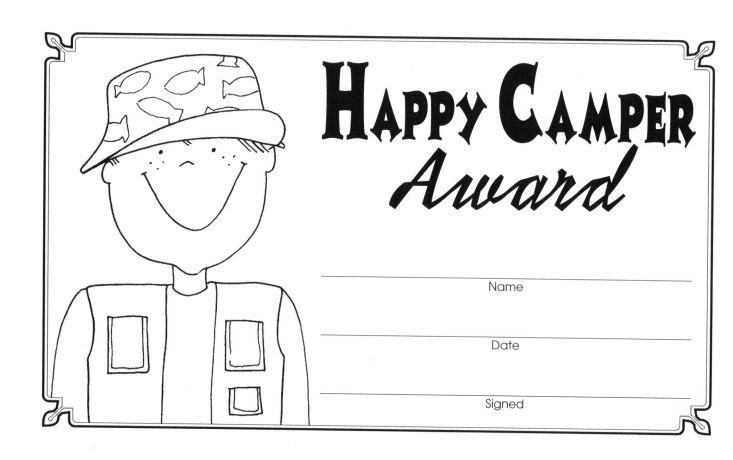

HAPPY CAMPER
Award

_____
Name

_____
Date

_____
Signed

SCIENCE AWARD

Name_____

Date_____

Signed_____

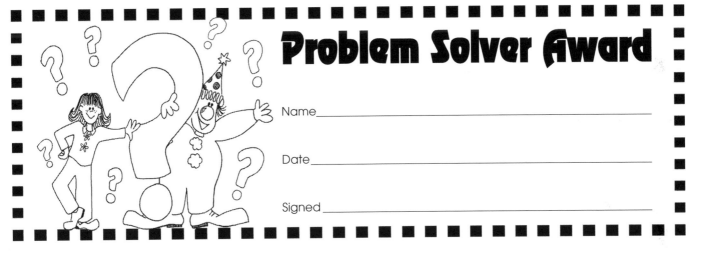

Problem Solver Award

Name_____

Date_____

Signed_____

MAGNIFICENT!

Name_____

Date_____

Signed_____

SUPER SPELLING!

Name_____

Date_____

Award Given For _____

Signed _____

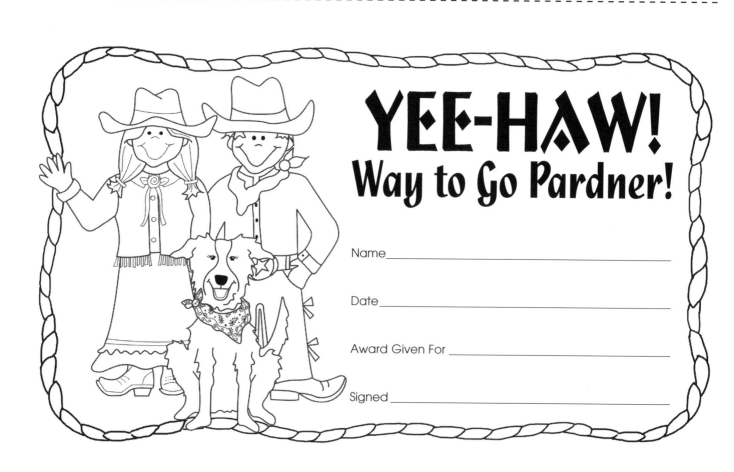

YEE-HAW!
Way to Go Pardner!

Name_____

Date_____

Award Given For _____

Signed _____

_____
Name

I'm singing your praises today because

_____
Date

_____
Award Given For

_____
Signed

You're An "EGG"-STRA STRONG Speller!

_____
Name

_____
Date

_____
Signed

DINO-MITE READER!

Name_____

Date_____

Award Given For _____

Signed _____

TERRIFIC TEAMWORK!

Name_____

Date_____

Signed _____

Smart in Art!

_____
Name

_____
Date

_____
Signed

YOU DID YOUR BEST TODAY.
Thank You!

_____
Name

_____
Date

_____
Signed

Music Award

_____
Name

_____
Date

_____
Signed

Your Handwriting is Bloomin' Good!

_____
Name

_____
Date

_____
Signed

COOL WORK!

_____
Name

_____
Date

_____
Signed

Lost a Tooth!

_____
Name

_____
Date

_____
Signed

Impressive
ART WORK!

Name_____

Date_____

Signed_____

You caught on quick
today in math!
WAY TO GO!

Name_____

Date_____

Signed_____

BIG IMPROVEMENT!

Name_____

Date_____

Signed_____

SMART THINKING!

You had your thinking cap on today during

_____

Name_____

Date_____

Signed_____

You were a "Honey" to have in my class! Thank you for making this year so special.

To _____

From _____

Date _____

CONGRATS!

To a smart "school of fish"

Name _____

finished _____ grade!

Date _____

Signed _____

You are
a real sweetie.

Happy
Valentines Day!

_____
To

_____
From

Happy
St. Patrick's Day!

_____
To

_____
From

Happy Easter

To

From

Celebrate!
It's the 4th of July!

To

From

HAPPY HALLOWEEN!

TRICK OR TREAT

You're a "TREAT" to have in my class!

To _____

From _____

Happy Thanksgiving

To _____

From _____

Happy Holidays!

To _____

From _____

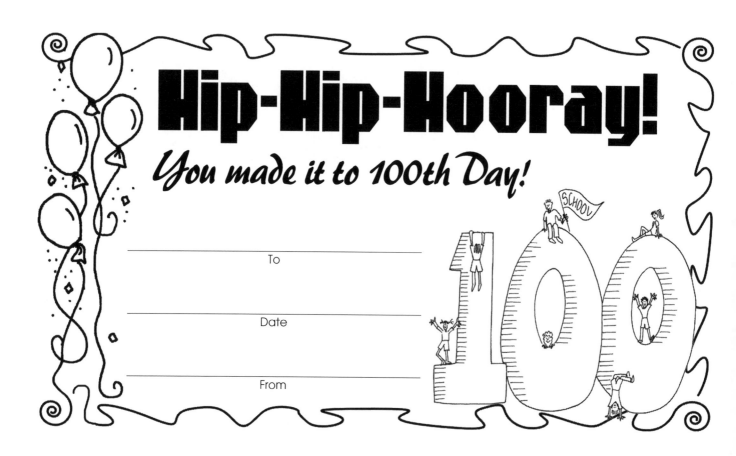

Hip-Hip-Hooray!

You made it to 100th Day!

_____
To

_____
Date

_____
From

Celebrate!
Today is Your Birthday

_____
To

_____
Date

_____
From

I'm so glad
that you were born!
Happy Birthday!

_____
To

_____
Date

_____
From

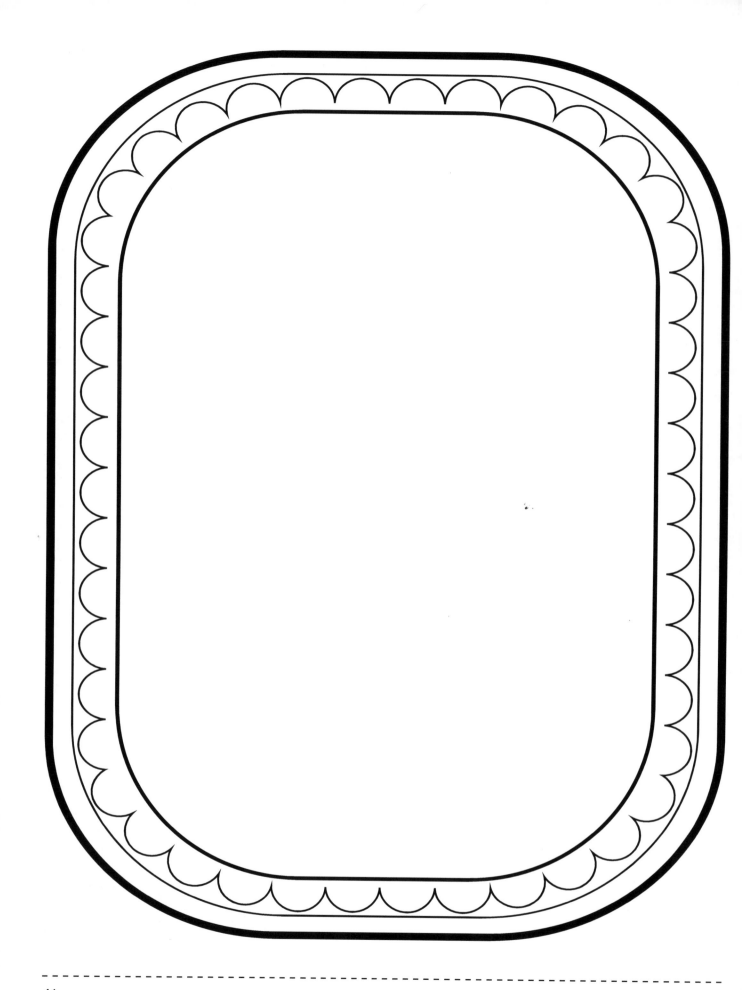

Made in the USA
Middletown, DE
31 March 2022

63445113R00029